ABCs

OF WISCONSIN

Dori Hillestad Butler ▪ Illustrations by Alison Relyea

TRAILS BOOKS
Black Earth, Wisconsin

Library of Congress Catalog Card Number: 99-69809

ISBN: 0-915024-79-9

Editor: Stan Stoga
Cover design: Kathie Campbell

Printed in China by Everbest Printing Co., Ltd.

06 05 04 03 02   6 5 4 3 2

Trails Media Group, Inc.
P.O. Box 317 • Black Earth, WI 53515
(800) 236-8088 • e-mail: info@wistrails.com
www.trailsbooks.com

Aa

Andrew awakes on the Apostle Islands.

Becky and Ben buy a Badger.

Bb

Cc

Courtney counts cows.

David discovers the Dells.

Dd

Ee

Elizabeth eyes the eagles.

Freddie follows the fish. Ff

Gg

Garrett and Gail grow grains.

Hannah houses honeybees.

Hh

Ii   Isaiah itches from ivy.

Jacob jumps for juice.

Jj

Kk

Kelly kayaks on the Kickapoo.

Lucas loves loons.

Ll

Mm

Megan makes maple syrup.

Noah naps in the North Woods.

Nn

Oo   Olivia outgrows her overalls.

Patrick pretends he's a Packer.

Pp

Qq

Quinn quietly quilts.

Roberto reaches for a robin.

Rr

Ss   Samantha slides in the snow.

Tanner and Tara trot down the trail.

Tt

Uu   Ursula uncovers underground treasures.

Valerie views violets.

Vv

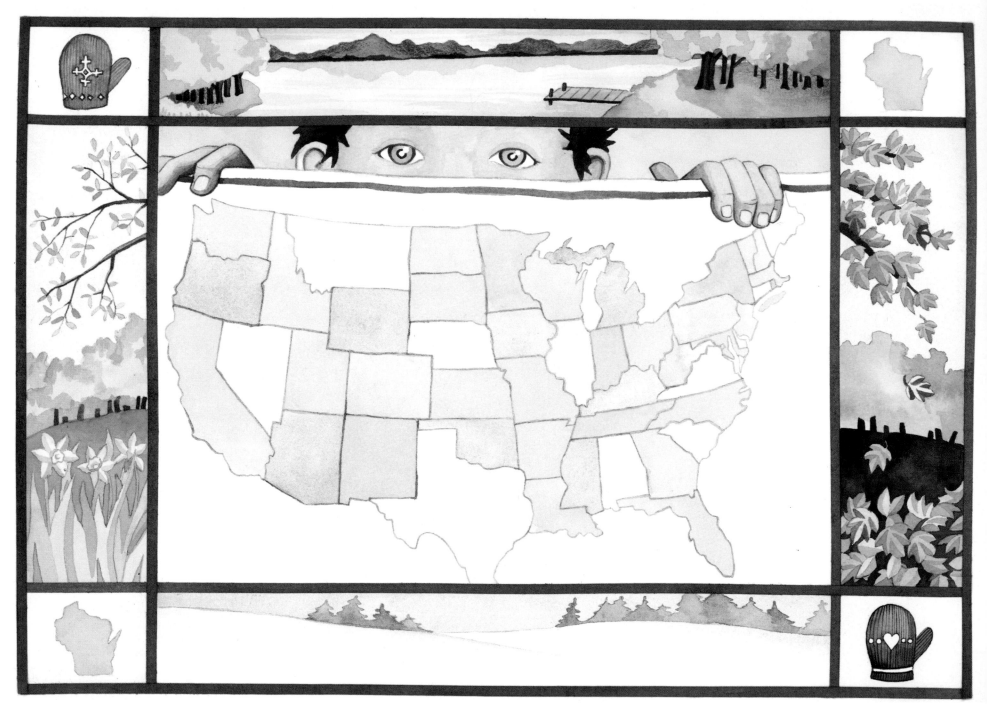

Ww

Will wonders, "Where's Wisconsin?"

Xavier x-country skis.

Xx

Yy   Yolanda yells, "Yummy!"

Zeke and Zoe zonk out at the zoo. Zz

Some Fun Facts

A The Apostle Islands are Wisconsin's northernmost point. Located in Lake Superior, there are 22 Apostle Islands. Madeline Island is the only one that is inhabited year-round.

B Bucky Badger is the mascot of the University of Wisconsin-Madison. During the 1820s, Wisconsin lead miners were called Badgers because, like the furry animal, they lived in the holes they dug. Today, Wisconsin's nickname is the Badger State.

C There are approximately 1.5 million cows in Wisconsin. They produce about 3 billion gallons of milk per year. That's enough milk to provide every American with one quart per week annually.

D The unusual sandstone cliffs and canyons of the Wisconsin Dells were carved thousands of years ago when the Wisconsin glacier melted and water from glacial Lake Wisconsin rushed through the area. The Winnebago nation claimed that the Dells were formed when a giant serpent forced its way through solid rock. The Dells are one of Wisconsin's most popular tourist destinations.

E Bald eagles nest in tall trees along some of Wisconsin's lakes and rivers, especially in the southwestern part of the state. Adult bald eagles weigh between 8 and 14 pounds and have a wingspan of up to 8 feet. The bald eagle is our national symbol.

F The muskellunge (muskie) is Wisconsin's state fish. Most muskies average 2.3 to 4 feet in length and 5 to 36 pounds in weight, making them the largest fish in the pike family. Wisconsinites also fish for bass, perch, sturgeon, and trout in the state's 15,000 lakes, rivers, and streams.

G Corn is Wisconsin's leading field crop as well as the state grain. Native Americans grew corn in the Wisconsin area 1,100 years ago. Today, Wisconsin farmers also grow hay, oats, barley, and wheat.

H The honeybee is the Wisconsin state insect. There are 20,000 different bee species, but only the honeybee produces honey and/or wax in quantities large enough that people can use. The average honeybee produces about 1/12th of a teaspoon of honey during its lifetime.

I Poison ivy sometimes grows as a vine on trees and sometimes grows as a shrub on the ground. The plant has three glossy leaves and white flowers that bloom in early to mid summer. Oils from the leaves and stems can irritate your skin.

J Cranberries are native to Wisconsin and are the state's leading fruit crop. They grow on low evergreen vines in marshy areas. If properly tended, a single cranberry bog can produce fruit for 100 years.

K The Kickapoo River has sometimes been referred to as the world's most crooked river. It twists and turns for 125 miles through southwestern Wisconsin before emptying into the Wisconsin River. The word *kickapoo* means "he who goes here and then there."

L The common loon is one of the Earth's oldest living bird species. Loons have been around for 60 million years. Their mournful cries can be heard across quiet Wisconsin lakes most often at dusk or when a storm is approaching.

M The sugar maple is Wisconsin's state tree. In the winter, sugarmakers drill a small hole into a tree, insert a spout, and hang a bucket over the spout. When temperatures rise above freezing, the sap begins to flow. The sap is collected and taken to sugarhouses, where it is made into maple syrup.

N The North Woods area of Wisconsin is known for its lakes, trees, and wildlife. You'll find more animals here than people. During the 1800s, this region was covered by forest, but by 1900 most of the trees had been cut down. Today, more trees are planted each year than are cut down.

O A Wisconsin company, Oshkosh B'Gosh has been making clothing since 1895. Originally, the company manufactured bib overalls for farmers and railroad workers. But in the early 1900s, it began making children's coveralls so that youngsters could dress like their fathers.

P The Green Bay Packers were formed in 1919 when the Indian Packing Company agreed to sponsor a local professional football team. Today, they're owned by the city of Green Bay. They're the only community-owned professional football team in the country.

Q Wisconsin winters are long and cold, so many people like to curl up with a heavy quilt to keep warm. The average January temperature is 14 degrees Fahrenheit. On January 24, 1922, thermometers in Danbury, Wisconsin, dropped to –54 degrees Fahrenheit, the lowest temperature ever recorded in the state.

R The robin is Wisconsin's state bird. In 1926, Wisconsin schoolchildren voted to select a state bird. The robin won in every county except Sheboygan (which voted for the bluebird), but it wasn't officially adopted as the state bird until Wisconsin's centennial in 1948.

S Wisconsin averages around 47 inches of snow each winter, but parts of northern Wisconsin may receive up to 100 inches during one season. In January 1904, Neillsville, Wisconsin, received 26 inches of snow in one day.

T Wisconsin contains hundreds of hiking, biking, skiing, and snowmobile trails. The most famous, the Ice Age Trail, winds through many regions of the state. It traces the farthest advance of the last glacier in Wisconsin. When the trail is complete, it will be 1,000 miles long.

U There are more than 300 known caves in Wisconsin, but only 4 are commercial establishments open to the public. The stalactites and stalagmites that you find inside caves are actually deposits of calcium carbonate. Stalactites grow down from the roof, and stalagmites grow up from the floor. It takes 200 years for stalagmites and stalactites to grow just one inch.

V The wood violet Is Wisconsin's state flower. On Arbor Day in 1908, Wisconsin schoolchildren chose four candidates to be the state flower—the violet, the wild rose, the water lily, and the arbutus. Exactly one year later, the children voted again. The violet received 67,178 out of 147,918 votes, but it wasn't officially adopted as the state flower until Wisconsin's centennial in 1948.

W The Wisconsin Territory was formed on July 3, 1836. It included present-day Wisconsin, Minnesota, Iowa, and even part of the Dakotas. On May 29, 1848, Wisconsin became the 30th state in the Union, and the borders were changed to what they are today.

X There are more than 350 cross-country skiing facilities in Wisconsin. One of the most popular cross-county ski races in the world is the Birkebeiner, which is run between Hayward and Cable every February.

Y Wisconsin is the nation's leader in the production of milk, cheese, and butter. Two Rivers, Wisconsin, claims to be the "Home of the Ice Cream Sundae." Legend has it that the frozen treat was first created there at Ed Berner's Ice Cream Parlor in 1881.

Z The Milwaukee County Zoo was founded in 1882. It was among the first zoos in the country in which the animals were not caged. Today, more than 2,500 animals make it their home.

More Great Titles from Trails Books

W Is for Wisconsin, *Dori Hillestad Butler and Eileen Dawson*

Wisconsin: The Story of the Badger State, *Norman K. Risjord*

Wisconsin Portraits: 55 People Who Made a Difference, *Martin Hintz*

Paddling Illinois: 64 Great Trips by Canoe and Kayak, *Mike Svob*

Bountiful Wisconsin: 110 Favorite Recipes, *Terese Allen*

Foods That Made Wisconsin Famous, *Richard J. Baumann*

Great Wisconsin Restaurants, *Dennis Getto*

Great Wisconsin Taverns: 101 Distinctive Badger Bars, *Dennis Boyer*

Great Minnesota Walks: 49 Strolls, Rambles, Hikes, and Treks, *Wm. Chad McGrath*

Creating a Perennial Garden in the Midwest, *Joan Severa*

The Spirit of Door County: A Photographic Essay, *Darryl R. Beers*

Up North Wisconsin: A Region for All Seasons, *Sharyn Alden*

The W-Files: True Reports of Wisconsin's Unexplained Phenomena, *Jay Rath*

The M-Files: True Reports of Minnesota's Unexplained Phenomena, *Jay Rath*

The I-Files: True Reports of Illinois's Unexplained Phenomena, *Jay Rath*

Great Wisconsin Walks: 45 Strolls, Rambles, Hikes, and Treks, *Wm. Chad McGrath*

Great Weekend Adventures, *the Editors of Wisconsin Trails*

Best Canoe Trails of Southern Wisconsin, *Michael E. Duncanson*

County Parks of Wisconsin: 600 Parks You Can Visit Featuring 25 Favorites, *Jeannette and Chet Bell*

The Wisconsin Traveler's Companion: A Guide to Country Sights, *Jerry Apps and Julie Sutter-Blair*

Walking Tours of Wisconsin's Historic Towns, *Lucy Rhodes, Elizabeth McBride, and Anita Matcha*

Portrait of the Past: A Photographic Journey Through Wisconsin 1865–1920, *Howard Mead, Jill Dean, and Susan Smith*

Paddling Northern Wisconsin, *Mike Svob*

Barns of Wisconsin, *Jerry Apps*

Best Wisconsin Bike Trips, *Phil Van Valkenberg*

Trails Books
P.O. Box 5650, Madison, WI 53705   (800) 236-8088   e-mail: info@wistrails.com   www.trailsbooks.com